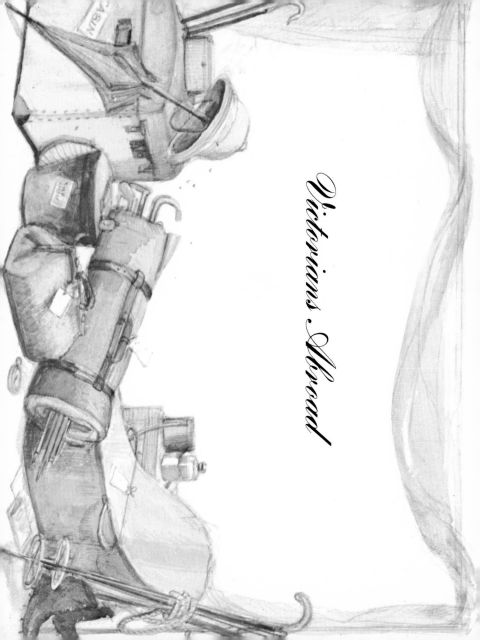

Victorians Abroad

Victorians Abroad

BY

John S. Goodall

ISBN 0 333 28453 4

First Published 1980 by MACMILLAN LONDON LIMITED
4 Little Essex Street London WC2R 3LF and Basingstoke, Associated companies
in New York Dublin Melbourne Johannesburg and Delhi.

Reproduced in Great Britain by Sackville Press Billericay Limited

Printed in Hong Kong

Victorians Abroad

John G. Goodall

Note

This book shows the English travelling abroad at various times during Victoria's long reign. The first pages depict the Grand Tour in the 1840s and the last ones a voyage to India in the 1890s. The order of the pictures and the subjects they represent are as follows:

Departure from England (title-page); Customs; French café; Switzerland; Crossing the Alps; Venice; Florence, the Uffizi Gallery; Rome; Pompeii; Biarritz; Paris, shopping; Versailles; Paris, Closerie des Lilas; Montmartre; Nice, Avenue Masséna; Monte Carlo; Deauville; Evian, taking the waters; Dresden, finishing school; Egypt, the Pyramids; Egypt, the Nile; Africa, exploration; Ship to India; Disembarking at Bombay; The Gymkhana Club; Calcutta, Viceregal Garden Party; Kashmir, the Dal Lake; Camping in the Kulu Valley; Simla; Malta, barn dance on a battleship; Dover.

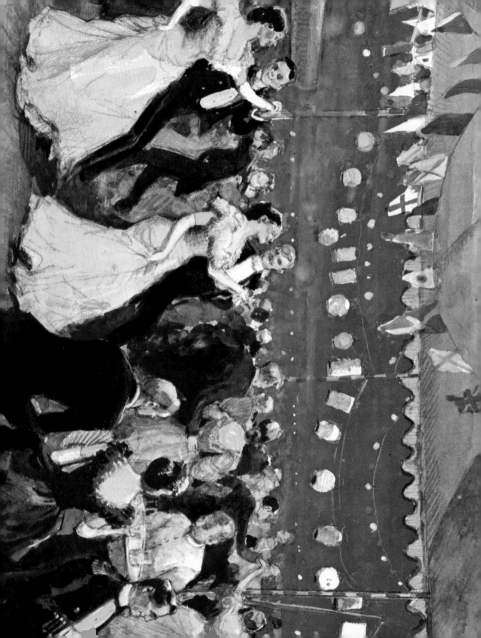